Make A List

First Printing, 2017

When you're feeling overwhelmed
and need to get things done,

Take a moment,
MAKE A LIST,
then check them off
one-by-one.

You have so many things to do
and don't want to forget.

See them on a piece of paper,
you'll get them done I bet!

You're heading to the grocery store and need supplies for dinner.

MAKE A LIST
of the food you need,
and you'll check out a winner!

GROCERY
LIST

1. Eggs
2. MILK
3. Sauce (tomato)
4. Bacon
5. yogurt
6. fruit
7. vegetables
8. Bread

Summer Wish List:

- [ ] Pool Time
- [x] Sleepover
- [ ] Camp
- [ ] Go to the beach
- [x] July Fourth
- [ ] Creativity
- [ ] Reading
- [x] Hang Out With Friends
- [ ] Go to the Movies
- [x] Sports
- [x] Birthday Parties
- [ ] Color and draw

Summer vacation is
around the corner,
there's so much fun in store!

MAKE A LIST of things to do
and you will get to more.

Your family wants to take a trip,
vacation or car ride.

MAKE A LIST together,
it will help you all decide.

Family Vacations

- [x] Beach house
- [x] N.C. zoo
- [ ] Disney World
- [ ] The Mountains

After school list

- ☐ Unpack backpack
- ☐ Do homework
- ☐ Read for 30 minutes
- ☐ Practice instrument
- ☐ Clean Room

Your mom gave you a
list of chores
to finish before you play.

Checking them off will
feel so good
that you will shout
HURRAY!

When you have some time
and you are not sure what to do,

MAKE A TOP TEN LIST
of your favorites to review.

Favorite Games

1. Chess
2. Codemaster
3. Ticket to ride
4. Clue
5. Checkers
6. Magic
7. Chocolate fix
8. Monopoly
9. Zingo
10. Bingo

Birthday List

1. battle masters

2. Ninjago lego sets

3. tree house

4. lego toy Pythore

5. ninja costume
   with a black belt

Your birthday is almost here
and you're not sure what to ask for.

MAKE A BIRTHDAY LIST
of toys from your favorite store.

Making lists is fun and quick,
try it and you'll see.

And when a check goes on your list,
so happy you will be!

BEACH LIST

- Swim Suit
- Buckets/Shovels
- S

MAKE A LIST

- ☐ Birthday List
- ☐ Christmas List
- ☐ Wish List
- ☐ To-do List
- ☐ Summer Bucket List
- ☐ Daily Chore List
- ☐ Grocery List
- ☐ Family Vacation List
- ☐ Dream Vacation List
- ☐ Top Ten List
    - ☐ Books
    - ☐ Games
    - ☐ Movies
    - ☐ Songs
    - ☐ Teams
    - ☐ Food
    - ☐ Cars
    - ☐ Toys

www.ingramcontent.com/pod-product-compliance
Lightning Source LLC
Chambersburg PA
CBHW040304100426
42811CB00011B/1358

You've Got
to
Have
FRIENDS

Delbert George FitzPenfield Anthony

You've Got to Have Friends

Illustrated by Rebecca Danielle Kimber

Passion To Profit Publishing
Montreal, Quebec

Published in: 2016 Delbert George FitzPenfield Anthony

Library and Archives Canada Cataloguing in Publication

Anthony, Delbert George FitzPenfield, author
        You've got to have friends / written by Delbert George FitzPenfield
Anthony ; drawings by Rebecca Danielle Kimber.

Issued in print and electronic formats.
ISBN 978-0-9936843-7-1 (softcover).--ISBN 978-0-9936843-8-8 (hardcover).--
ISBN 978-0-9936843-9-5 (PDF)

        1. Friendship--Juvenile literature. I. Kimber, Rebecca Danielle, illustrator
II. Title.

BF575.F66A58 2016   j158.2'5   C2016-907942-2
                                                         C2016-907943-0

Passion To Profit Publishing
www.passiontoprofitinc.com
Montreal, Quebec, Canada

Acknowledgements
Cover Design by Gordan Blazevic (gordan.blazevic@gmail.com)
Illustrations by Rebecca Danielle Kimber

Debra Dedyluk, Kevin Pendergraft, Dwightford Anthony senior, Durward Anthony, Alpha Mansaray, Peter Jacob and Rupert Benson for lending a friendly ear during the publication of this book.

WHEN WE LIVE FROM OUR **heart**, WE ARE **kind**

and

WHEN WE ARE **kind**, WE ARE **friendly**.

FRIENDS ARE LIKE STUFFED ANIMALS,

CAKES, COOKIES AND CANDLES;

SOME ARE **sweet** AND **nutty**.

AND OTHERS ARE

huggable AND **loveable**.

AND OTHERS ARE

God-like.

SOME FRIENDS ARE

winers AND OTHERS ARE **diners**.

SOME ARE **thinkers**
AND OTHERS ARE **finkers**.
SOME ARE **hard**
AND OTHERS ARE **mushy**.

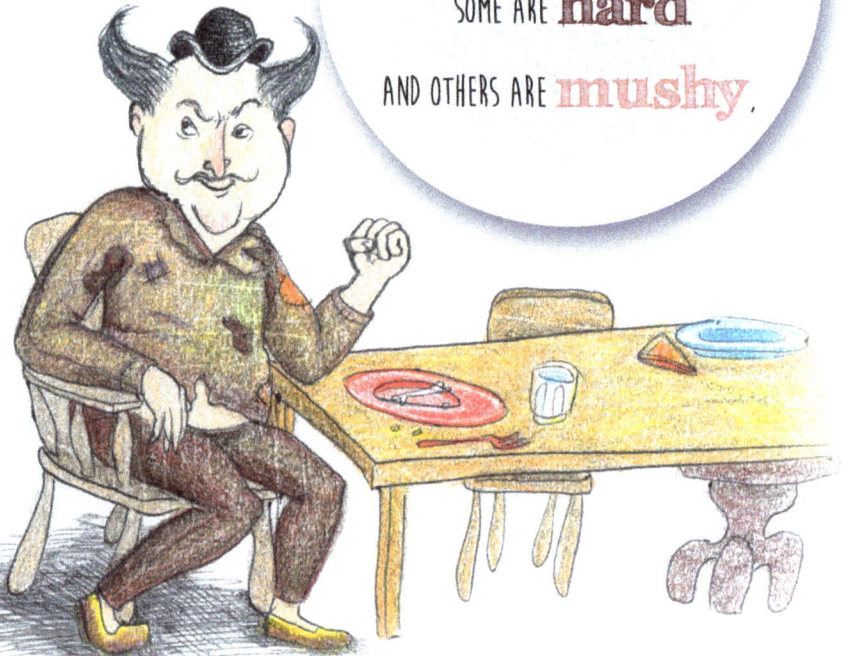

SOME FRIENDS ARE

thankful AND OTHERS ARE

abusers

SOME FRIENDS ARE
tiny AND SOME ARE
fReAky.

SOME ARE homey
AND OTHERS ARE lonely.

SOME ARE happy
AND SOME ARE
zappy

SOME ARE
tacky.

BUT
YOU'VE GOT
TO
HAVE
FRIENDS

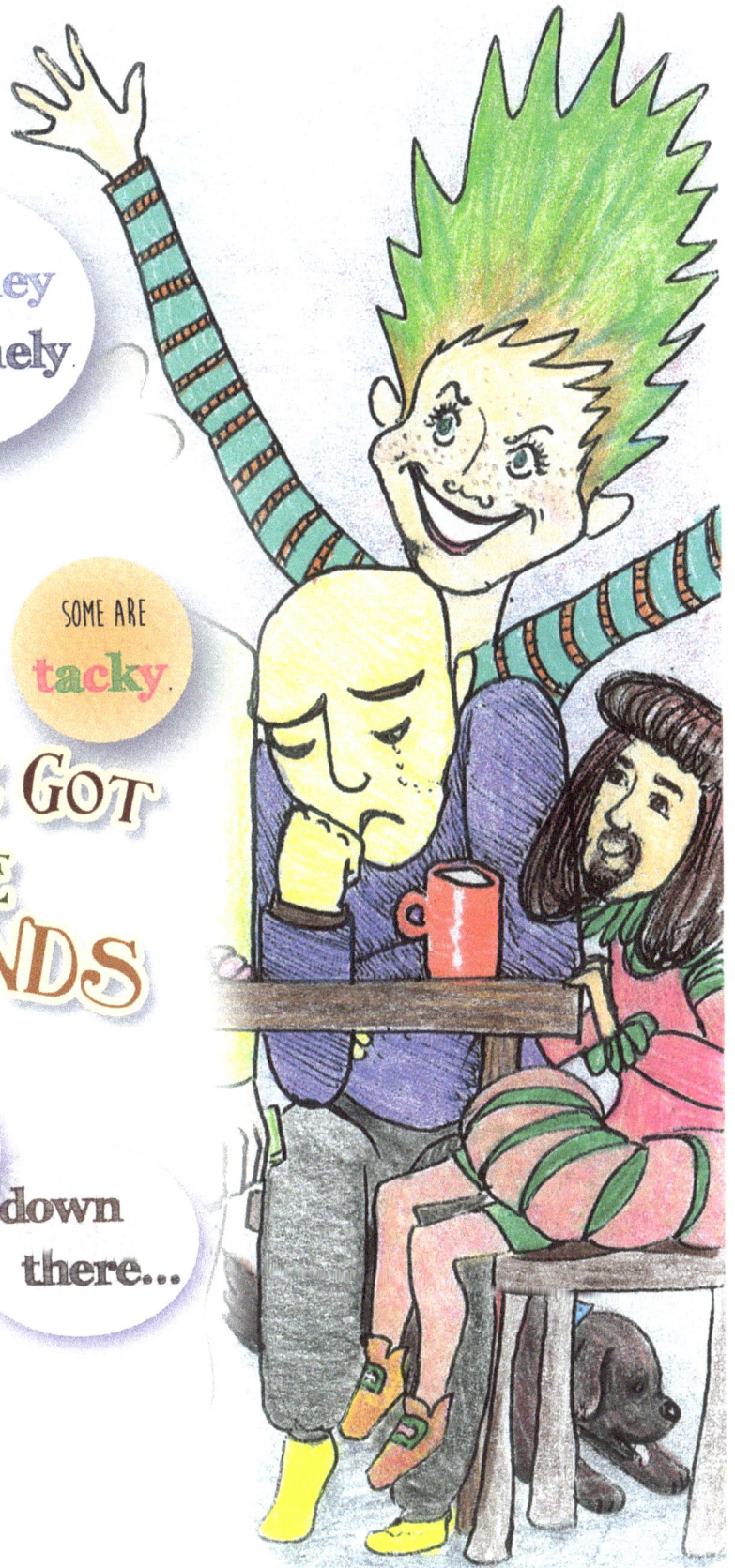

SOME ARE FROM Utopia
AND OTHERS ARE FROM
down
there...

BUT
YOU'VE GOT
TO
HAVE
FRIENDS

SOME ARE great chefs AND OTHERS ARE burger-snatchers.

SOME ARE dreamers AND SOME ARE dream-takers.

SOME FRIENDS ARE full of bologna AND OTHERS ARE vegetarians.

BUT You've Got TO HAVE FRIENDS

SOME ARE
unforgettable
AND SOME ARE
unbelievable,

SOME ARE
religious
AND SOME ARE
spiritual,

SOME SUFFER FROM
gloomania

AND SOME SUFFER FROM
ENTHUSIASM

BUT
YOU'VE GOT TO HAVE FRIENDS

SOME ARE **artistic**

AND SOME ARE A

work of art,

SOME ARE **rich**

AND SOME ARE **poor**,

SOME ARE AS

BRIGHT

AS SUNSHINE

WHILE SOME ARE AS

beautiful

AS SNOWFLAKE.

BUT

YOU'VE GOT TO HAVE FRIENDS

SOME ARE

full of B.O.

Some friends give you a **pinch** or **two**, a **dash** for the **cash** or the **door**.

Or simply give you a **smile** and a **chuckle**,

or a **tear of joy**, a **shake** or a **frown**. A **squeeze** or a **tease** and a **hug** instead of a **smack**,

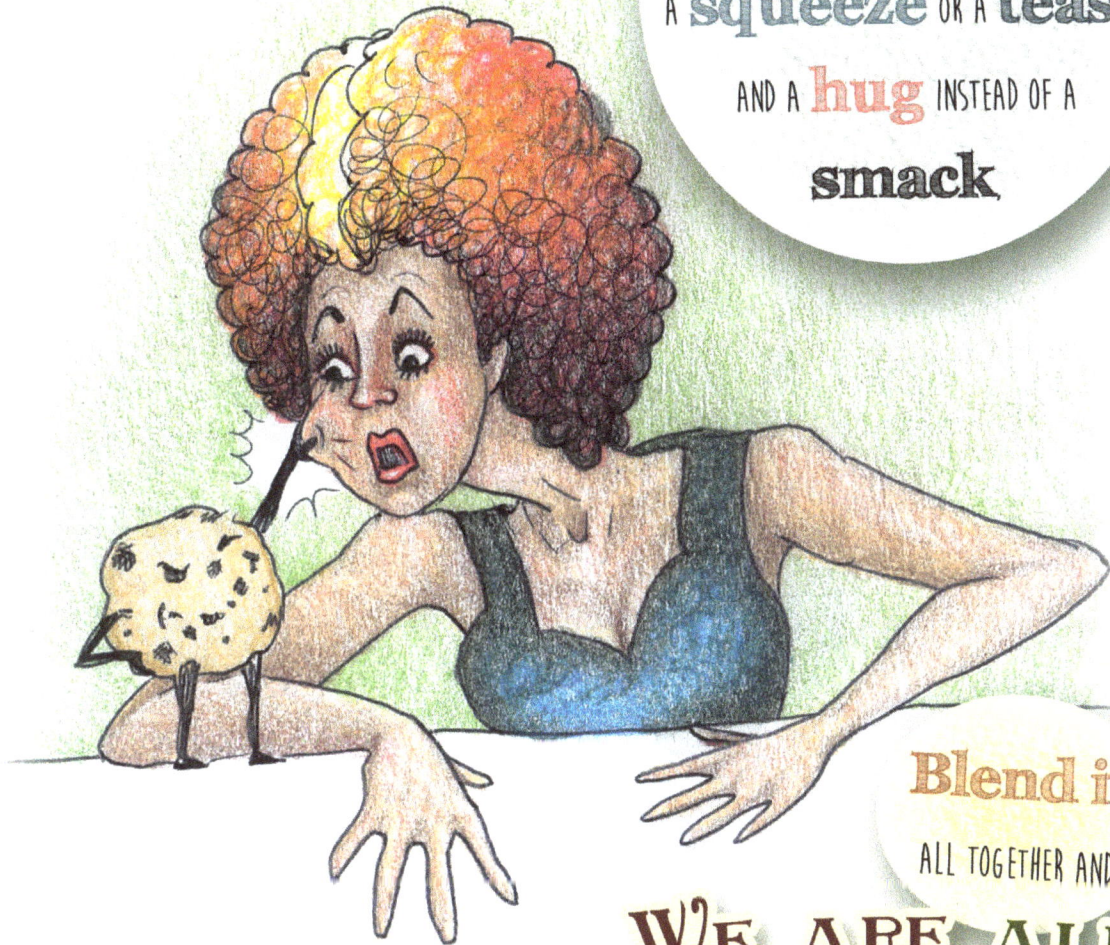

Blend it all together and

WE ARE ALL FRIENDS

IT'S NOT ABOUT THE

time frame,

IT'S ABOUT THE

mind frame.

This book is about You and Your friends!

To all our family, friends and associates we would like to thank all who have inspired us to create this book. Huge gratitude to Debra Dedyluk for connecting and supporting us through the creation of this book. Delbert and Rebecca both acknowledge and give gratitude towards the lessons of friendship built throughout the construction of this manuscript. The experience we have had while creating this book has truly demonstrated that *We've Got to Have Friends*.

"I would call this a friendly, family book for ALL." ~Debra Dedyluk

It's not about the time frame, it's about the mind frame.

WRITER'S DEDICATION:

I personally dedicate this book to the following family and friends: my Aunts Pauline and Minerva Neblette, my cousin Andrea Price, Terrence Campbell; (my best friend since kindergarten/"first standard") and Ariel Ashley. To the many friendships I had with my parents (Dr. Desmond Anthony Senior and Eileen Anthony) before they passed on. A very special thanks belongs to my life coach, Tee Crane and another thank you to everyone from *Unity in Action*. Without their friendship of respect, honesty and integrity, I would not be able to acknowledge the meaning of true friendship. *From my heart to all hearts, may we develop and create friendships from the start.*

ARTIST'S DEDICATION:

I dedicate the drawings/illustrations to Delbert and his commitment to living his truth. I admire and support his dedication to humanity; togetherness and spiritual/creative expression. The painting to the right was made alongside this book and touches on many of the underlying themes and concepts of friendship.

Face of Peaceful Faces
acrylic on canvas, 9"x 11", 2016

www.ingramcontent.com/pod-product-compliance
Lightning Source LLC
Chambersburg PA
CBHW040304100426
42811CB00011B/1359